Mark Wheeller

Chicken!

A Theatre-in-Education play for older people to perform for a Key Stage 2 audience

Salamander Street

PLAYS

First published by dbda in 1992 under the title *Why did the Chicken Cross the Road?*; Updated and reprinted in 2003; *Chicken!* was first published in 2006 and further revised and updated in 2014 & 2017 ISBN 9781902843193

This new edition (revised and updated again) first published in 2020 by Salamander Street Ltd., 272 Bath Street, Glasgow, G2 4JR (info@salamanderstreet.com)

PB ISBN: 9781913630331
E ISBN: 9781913630324

Cover and text design by Konstantinos Vasdekis

10 9 8 7 6 5 4 3 2 1

Further copies of this publication can be purchased from www.salamanderstreet.com

CONTENTS

Acknowledgements

Thanks to StopWatchTheatre Company for their outstanding production of this play, since 1992, and now to Wizard Theatre who continue professional performances in the UK.

Cassie Eccles; Chris Gilfoy; Lizzie Hole; Kirsty Housley; Matthew Simpson; Samantha Phillips; Paul Sturrock; Carley Wilson; all students at Oaklands Community School who assisted in developing the original opening section, improvised from my storyline. This scene was re-written by Chris Gilfoy, Matthew Simpson, Samantha Phillips and Mark Wheeller, for the 2003 version of the play.

I should also like to thank Karmin Arnold, Lewis Evans, Ross Hobby & Emily Moulsdale for their help in updating the 2017 version of the script during the rehearsal process for the Victoria Shanghai Academy performances.

Headteacher and staff at Sinclair and Oakwood Middle Schools, Southampton (1998).

Rachael Wheeller, for numerous proofreadings and general tolerance.

John Askew, Local Authority Road Safety Officers' Association.

Carol Bagshaw, Hampshire County Council.

Martin Ryves, Headteacher, Worton Junior School.

Adrian New and Steven Pearce and the actors from StopWatch Theatre Company.

Leon Hamilton and all those at Wizard Theatre.

Dr. Peter Hollis, formerly Headteacher, Oaklands Community School.

Dbda who later became Zinc for making the play available in the first place and through until 2020.

Thanks to George Spender and those in the Salamander Street team for their efforts to extend the reach of my plays.

Sophie Gorell Barnes of MBA Literary Agents for their continued support of my work.

Foreword

I have worked in Theatre in Education for thirty years, and *Chicken!* has been a part of that for twenty-eight of them.

StopWatch Theatre Company was the resident TiE company at Oaklands Community School in Southampton where Mark Wheeller had generously offered us a base in return for our input to the drama curriculum and youth theatre. He had plans for his new road safety play to be performed to local junior schools in the Summer of 1992 and asked us to write and deliver a workshop to accompany the performance.

The play and workshop were really well received, not just by the schools but by the hordes of Road Safety Officers who were fans of *Too Much Punch for Judy* and had travelled from across the UK to see it. They were all desperate to see it performed in their schools, and before we knew it we had a seven week tour booked for November and December 1992, plus an invitation to perform at a series of regional conferences which would allow a representative of every local authority in Great Britain to see it. By the end of those conferences we were sold out for a year and *Chicken!* was firmly established as an exciting new programme in schools across the land.

This success continued for eighteen years, until sadly austerity drastically reduced the number of local authorities who were able to afford "luxuries" like TiE. Although reduced to a handful, there are still those who believe in the benefits of TiE to affect attitudes and behaviours for the better and continue to support our visits to their schools. I am so grateful to all of them over the years for their support.

But the play we performed in 1992 had substantial differences to the script you are holding now. And I attribute part of the longevity of the programme to the fact that we have constantly reviewed and revised the script to keep up with both road safety priorities and cultural references.

The first thing you would notice about the original script is that the central characters were both boys (Chris and Matt) rather than the boy and girl (Chris and Tammy) that we have today. That change, with the knock on impact for doubling in a 2M, 2F cast, was central to the first major rewrite which happened in 1998. We took our thoughts about the need for change to Mark who gamely rewrote the script to make this work, and it made a big change for the better to audience responses straight away.

Changes in technology have also been referenced over time, both incidental and central to the story. For example the gift of desire from Aunt Ermintrude has cycled through Tamagotchis (ask your parents!) Gameboys, PlayStations, Xboxs, iPods and iPhones. But more important than that, the nature of the threat from the dare was raised with filming on "camera phones" and then ultimately to putting on YouTube.

More incidental and off the cuff references are always updated from production to production, mentioning current TV shows or pop stars where appropriate. And the success of the programme has been maintained by our willingness to keep it fresh.

The last significant rewrite in 2018 came in response to the realisation that audiences were suddenly no longer responding well to the good natured banter centred on boys and girls. Innocently conceived lines derived to get humour from a "battle of the sexes" between Chris and Tammy were now seen as contentious slurs, met with gasps rather than laughter. The #MeToo movement and the gender politics of the age were understood by the ten year olds we were performing to, and we acted quickly to rid the script of these outdated ideas.

At this point I have to credit the hundreds of actors (some of whom went on to direct teams) who have made this production their own over the years, and used their skill and passion to drive the show forward. I always send a new team on the road with the idea that they are the torch bearers for the next few months, and their creativity and experience is welcome to make the show as good as it can be every day, and they are encouraged to try new things. That is when the show is most successful, when those who perform it properly own it, and I would encourage you, whether performing the whole script, or just a scene in the classroom, to do the same. Play with it, have fun, make it your own and continue the legacy which has enthralled over half a million children over the last twenty-eight years.

Adrian New
Producer, StopWatch Theatre Company
May 2020

Introduction

If, in 1986, had I set out to write my "hit" play it would not have been a road safety play. No one is more surprised than me, at the enormous success achieved by *Too Much Punch for Judy* which was initially a twenty-minute end section to a youth theatre play, ostensibly about alcohol abuse. *Too Much Punch* toured in the UK from 1987 through to 2018.[1] In 1991, I was awarded the Prince Michael of Kent Special Award for Services to Road Safety Education. It was, in part, this award which inspired the idea of a play for an upper Junior/lower Secondary age group.

I contacted a number of Road Safety Officers across the country to ask their advice as to what sort of issues such a play should cover. An officer in Hertfordshire suggested that I hold a meeting with teachers from the schools where we planned to perform the play, to find out what their concerns were.

I followed his advice and in the meeting, I discovered great enthusiasm on the part of these teachers for the idea of a new road safety play. Issues were put forward, many that I had not previously considered. One in particular was common to both schools who were part of the trial for the play – the game of "Chicken", where children dare each other to cross the road in front of oncoming traffic. There had already been a death as a result of this problem at one of the schools.

I have to confess that I had gone into this meeting expecting the major issue to be the use of cycle helmets, although I was aware that Hampshire had done a lot of work promoting cycle safety. It transpired that cycle safety issues were far broader than just cycle helmets (although still only a small number of children actually wore them), and the teachers wanted me to try and incorporate a range of basic "safety tips" for cyclists.

I returned home and worked on an outline story for the play, which my Monday afternoon extracurricular drama group would improvise the following week. I can't say that I spent hours slaving over a hot word processor, but I thought about it a lot. Gradually, the story took shape.

---

1 Full details in the introduction for *Too Much Punch for Judy*.

I decided to use the idea I originally had… that of the cycle helmet story, as a red herring, leading the audience to believe that one of the two central characters would be killed as a result of refusing to wear the helmet. Then, at the end there would be a twist, leading to the other character being hit by a car after being called a "chicken".

I showed the Monday group on outline of this idea and asked them to devise a lively scene showing the lead up to a Christmas Day on which two friends (later cousins) were both given a bike and a helmet. By the end of the scene, their differing attitudes to cycle helmets should be apparent.

The group came back with two improvisations. The best bits from each formed the opening scene for this new play. I was delighted, it was pacey and full of energy! Although characters and ideas were developed in subsequent meetings, with time running out, I took on the task of writing the remaining scenes in the tradition of slaving over a hot word processor.

When my rather hurried draft of my script had been printed we had precisely two weeks until our first performance. We booked a room and rehearsed almost every evening during that period. Everyone worked unbelievably hard and lots of imaginative ideas helped to present this play in the round (which was new to all the cast and greeted with much suspicion!) and (as was intended with this multi-location/zero budget play) without the use of any props… except two cycle helmets!

I felt that the play needed some kind of follow-up. However, we did not have time to devise and rehearse a workshop. Hampshire County Council Road Safety Unit and the County Road Safety Officers Association came to our rescue by funding our school's (then) resident StopWatch Theatre Company, to devise and run participatory workshops for all the 8-12 year olds who were to see the play.

The title was the final thing to happen. Our working title was *Dean and Danny*, the original names of the two central characters. This was hated by almost all who heard it. When I come up with *Why Did The Chicken Cross The Road?* (the title of this play in its first incarnation) I almost dismissed it… but slowly it grew on me and, when other people thought it was "right", the Monday group gave their seal of approval and so the title was finally adopted (and before it was shortened it was lengthened to become *Why Did The Chicken Cross the Road? Because Some Stupid Turkey Egged Her On!*)

The performances went down really well. The children were gripped and many of the adults who came to see it (we encouraged parents to attend) were in tears! A large number of Road Safety Officers, from all over England came to see the production. All left wanting it to be presented professionally in their areas – except, bizarrely, those in our own county of Hampshire who, ironically, remain to this day one of the very few English counties never to have used the play!

StopWatch Theatre Company expressed a serious interest in touring the play professionally. Their ideas, coupled with various hints I had gleaned from Road Safety Officers following the initial performances, led to the second and much more developed version of this play being written.

Why Did The Chicken Cross The Road? has almost outdone its predecessor *Too Much Punch For Judy*. It has been performed magnificently by StopWatch Theatre Company. In total, it has been performed 5,876 times (most of them by StopWatch) between 1992 and 2020, an average of nearly one every day since it was written – a better average than *Punch*! Their outstanding productions have helped the play to gain a reputation as one that is both educational in content and stylistically interesting to drama teachers and their students.

Five further radical rewrites have occurred since 1992. In 1997, StopWatch felt that the 8-13 year-olds of 1997 were more "grown up" than the 8-13 year-olds of 1992. Also we needed to encourage girls to empathise more closely with the central characters. So, Matt became Tammy! Matt's girlfriend became Tammy's boyfriend. Matt's mum became Tammy's dad so that the play would still work for a cast of 2 male and 2 female.

In 2006, I was inspired to update the play, when, amongst other 'upgrades' I had the idea of the "Chicken" dare being filmed on a mobile phone. In 2016 a number of factors dated the play so OYT and myself made further improvements and updates. Further changes were made in 2017 following the #MeToo movement.

The only similarity this new *Chicken!* has with the original 1992 play, is the basic sequence of events. Even the end is different from the earliest version of the touring play where the cousin was not killed but received a spinal injury. I guess one lesson to be taken from this is that no play (no matter how successful it may be) is ever "finished". Mine are always "works in progress".

Chicken! was written to be performed by any secondary school age group (ideally for a target audience of 8-12 year-olds. At my school in Southampton we used the opening scene as one of our "page to stage" exercises for Year 9 students to present. They enjoy the lively nature of the scene and the use of choral speech and choral movement proves to be an excellent teaching tool for this age group. My own children were amused to discover *Chicken!* was also on the school curriculum at their secondary school. Each of my three children had their own reactions to their dad being studied. Ollie didn't ever want attention drawn to it. Charlie was keen that everyone should know. Daisy waited until someone asked which they did jokingly saying:

"Is that your brother, Daisy?", and she replied quite proudly

"No, but he is my dad!"

Of course the person who questioned her didn't believe her, but the drama teacher (who I knew) verified the fact!

Good luck to all who attempt to perform this play. I hope that you will find it challenging and exciting to work on.

Mark Wheeller

Note: The play should be performed with minimum props and maximum imagination.

In 2019 I went to see one of the final StopWatch performances before Adrian retired from TiE (and passed it onto Wizard Theatre Company).

I wrote a review for my Wheellerplays Facebook page to acknowledge the contribution StopWatch have made to the popularity and longevity of this play.

Chicken! by StopWatch Theatre Company Spring Tour (2019).

Review by Mark Wheeller

It's always good to catch up with *Chicken!*. By the end of this tour, it will have been performed 5,836 times in its twenty-seven years, twenty-six of which has been consecutive professional touring. It is especially significant as it is the last tour StopWatch Theatre Company will present.

StopWatch, under the incredible leadership of Adrian New (& in the early years Steve Pearce) have presented all but a few this gigantic number.

The day I saw this production, another TiE company were in the audience hoping to adopt *Chicken!*, ensuring English schools continue to benefit from it.

Last time I saw it, the energy levels and humour took me by surprise. This time I was expecting that and I was not disappointed. The young audience were literally on the edge of their seats and vocal (which did take me by surprise), as they reacted to the characters actions. This added so much to the atmosphere.

I remember this happened to us when OYT performed it in Hong Kong, but I'd never seen this reaction in the UK. Apparently, it's a regular thing now! Excellent!

The other thing that took me by surprise was the tragedy at the end. It really tugged at the heartstrings and provided a beautiful contrast to the high energy set up.

StopWatch have done an incredible job, on what has become a uniquely successful play. At this distance of time, nearly thirty years, I can see why. It's lively, focussed, and the ending is deeply moving.

Thank you StopWatch for successfully bringing these qualities out in all your productions over the years and for encouraging me to review and renew it periodically. My writing is part of the story. The StopWatch production and their amazing performers are very much the other part. Thanks.

The power of that performance inspired the idea to make a DVD of the professional production so long after the production students studying my plays can see a uniquely successful TiE program.

This is the first professional production of any of my plays to be filmed.

You can purchase this complete programme (production, interactive workshop plus interviews with cast and production team) from the Salamander Street website.

Chris Gilfoy – from the original Oaklands Community School production – looking back on *Chicken!* but never imagining how things would turn out…

Having been involved in youth theatre for a few years I jumped at the chance when Mark approached me to help him with a new project. A group of us met once maybe twice a week bouncing ideas around and trying different scenarios… a lot of it was trial and error. There was lots of improvisation. Some ideas worked and some didn't! Once we had a basic road safety structure, *Chicken!* was born.

Originally the two main characters were called Dean and Danny but that quickly evolved into Chris (me) and Matt (Matt Simpson) we even used my Mum's real name, Ann as Chris's mum!

Initially, we used references such as Subbuteo and a Diamondback mountain bike. Both were very popular at the time we did the first draft (prior to the popularity of computer games).

Over the years I have seen *Chicken!* performed in many different ways, with lots of changes to make it more modern.

I'm pleased the Christmas scene has remained, since that was a piece we all originally devised.

It's been a real honour to see it taken on tour by a professional theatre company for many years, as I still consider *Chicken!* to be a part of me.

I never thought that many years on I would be back in the theatre watching a production based on MY actual life changing events…

Chris's story can be seen in what might be considered a partner play, **Chequered Flags to Chequered Futures**. *It's quite a story and an exciting and powerful play. Do take a look. You can find it on the Salamander Street website.*

The first version of this play was first performed by Oaklands Community School "Monday Group" on 22 June 1992 with the following cast:

Chris	Chris Gilfoy
Matt	Matthew Simpson
Ann	Kirsty Housley
Sue	Samantha Phillips
Shopkeeper	Angie Johnston
Ian Sturrock	Chris Claridge
Mate	Daniel Sturrock
Linda Ratcliffe	Cassie Eccles
Car Driver	Carly Wilson
Cyclist	Sarah Ridout

Other parts in the original version played by: Jensen Bourke, Lizzie Hole, Christion Onslow, Kelly Ridout, Paul Severn and Paul Sturrock.

The play received its first professional performance by the Southampton-based StopWatch Theatre Company in September 1992.

Characters

The play has 9 main characters: 4 male, 3 female and 2+ of either sex.

It can also be presented by 2 males and 2 females, in which case the cast should be as follows:

Doubling for Touring Version:

FEMALE 1
Tammy

FEMALE 2
Ann, The Massive, Liz

MALE 1
Chris, Nut-Job

MALE 2
Ray, Gary

Section 1

A BIKE FOR CHRISTMAS

As the audience arrive music is playing. Throughout the following scene the two families mirror each other on either side of the stage, representing their different homes.

CHRIS: *(With a high five.)* Chris!

TAMMY: *(With a high five.)* Tammy!

TAMMY & CHRIS: Cousins and best mates
Chillin' together on the local estates.

TAMMY: Water fights at weekends ...

CHRIS: ... playing knock-door-run

> **TAMMY** *becomes an irate neighbour as* **CHRIS** *knocks on her door. She freezes, shaking her fist at him, and as he runs away he uses his phone to take a selfie with her in the background.*

CHRIS: Selfie!

TAMMY: *(Breaking out of freeze and laughing.)* Filming what happens and always having fun!

CHRIS: Showing it to our mates next day makes everybody laugh.

TAMMY: But if your mum caught sight of them she'd drown you in the bath!

CHRIS: She's not that bad!

TAMMY: She's... *well* sad!

TAMMY & CHRIS: Anyway ...

TAMMY: Christmas is coming and there's one thing we'd both like ...

CHRIS: A state of the art ...

TAMMY: ... well sorted ...

TAMMY & CHRIS: ... mountain bike.

TAMMY: We've dropped some blatant hints

CHRIS: ... almost every day.

TAMMY & CHRIS: But if Mum/Dad's bought one, it's hidden well away.
(NB Throughout choral sections, Tammy says "Dad" and Chris says "Mum")

CHRIS: So a potted introduction has passed before your eye.

TAMMY & CHRIS: And here we are for you today… the "dramatis personae".

TAMMY: There is one little problem though… we're meant to be thirteen.

CHRIS: Easy… *(To audience.)* … suspend your disbelief in every single scene.
In Theatre you can conjure up anything at all.

TAMMY: Like what?

CHRIS: A microphone

TAMMY: DJ!

CHRIS: … Pump it Up!

TAMMY: … Good call!

They go into a DJ/rap routine. **TAMMY** *soon stops but* **CHRIS** *continues.*
Chris! *(The music stops.)*

CHRIS: At least I don't wear Peppa Pig pyjamas.

TAMMY: No, you wear Paw Patrol pyjamas!
Anyway we're here to do this play
So, let's introduce our folks …

TAMMY & CHRIS: … and get it underway.

CHRIS: My mum… Ann.

ANN: Hello! *(As if lighting up her face.)*

TAMMY: And my dad… Ray.

RAY: Hi! *(As if lighting up his face.)*

CHRIS & TAMMY: Come on Mum/Dad tell us, what's the date today?

RAY & ANN: 15th December.

ALL: Ten more days till Christmas!!!

TAMMY & CHRIS: Mum/Dad. I'd really like a bike for Christmas.

RAY & ANN: We'll see…

TAMMY & CHRIS: You always say *(Imitating.)* "We'll see".

RAY & ANN: Well! We'll see! Now time for bed!

TAMMY & CHRIS: Do I have to?

RAY & ANN: Yes… or do you want a goodnight kiss?

TAMMY & CHRIS: Yeuch! Maybe I will go to bed!

Exit.

RAY & ANN: iPad. Online shopping!
(They each grab an iPad – exaggerated mime – and open it.)
Best Bikes Dot Com.
(They point at the screen.)
That one! That one! That one!
(Finally they point at the same one.)
That one!!!

RAY: She'll be ever so pleased with it!

ANN: I can't wait for his little face to light up when he sees it.

RAY & ANN: Add to basket. Checkout. *(Reading in a questioning voice.)*
Please watch this safety video before you continue?

CHRIS *and* **TAMMY** *(or in a larger cast production two specific actors) play the presenters in a cheesy safety video. Equally cheesy music underscores the exaggerated mime style performances with the following voice over:*

Thanks for choosing Best Bikes Dot Com. We know you'll love your shiny new bicycle, but we want all our customers to be safe on those busy roads. So we've put together an essential safety pack, that no safety conscious rider should be without.
Light your way with these ultra-bright LED lights. Be safe, be seen!
Look super cool in this super bright clothing – high vis for the day with reflective strips for night.
Don't be a spanner! Never forget your tool kit – always be ready to fix those punctures and tighten your brakes.
And finally, the most important item no cyclist should ever be without. Theeeeeeeeeeee cycle helmet! Use your head, don't lose your head!
Just click below this video to add all these essential items to your order. Thanks for watching, and be safe out there! *(Freeze and exit.)*

RAY & ANN: Essential… we'll have the lot. Click!
(To audience.) Can't accuse us of not being safety conscious.
Checkout. Buy!

TAMMY & CHRIS:*(From offstage, they make the sound of ringing a doorbell)*
Bing bong!

RAY & ANN: Delivered! Garage…*(Opening the garage door upwards.)*
Hide the bike.

TAMMY & CHRIS: *(Offstage.)* Hi Mum/Dad. I'm home.

RAY & ANN: Oh no!

TAMMY & CHRIS: *(Lively entrance.)* Hi Mum/Dad. I'm home.
*(***RAY** *&* **ANN** *freeze. Silence.)*
Mum/Dad, where are you? *(They spot their parents.)*

RAY & ANN: Awkward!

TAMMY & CHRIS: What are you doing in the garage?

RAY & ANN: *(Whistling or singing to "cover" obvious guilt.)* Oh nothing!

TAMMY & CHRIS: What do you mean nothing?

RAY & ANN: Nothing to do with you.

Momentarily freeze action.

ALL: Five more days till Christmas!
Aaaaaargh! Shops are packed!

RAY & ANNE: *(Reading shopping list. As they do this* **CHRIS** *and* **TAMMY** *reach out and put said item into the trolley.)* Potatoes… Turkey… Carrots… Sprouts.

CHRIS & TAMMY: Yeuchh. Chocolate, chocolate, chocolate, chocolate!

ALL: Now the tree.

TAMMY & CHRIS: Tree. *(***TAMMY** *&* **CHRIS** *point out different trees, using the audience. As they do this* **ANN** *and* **RAY** *find a different fault.)*

RAY & ANN: Too small.

TAMMY & CHRIS: Tree.

RAY & ANN: Too tall.

TAMMY & CHRIS: Tree.

RAY & ANN: No needles.

TAMMY & CHRIS: Tree.

RAY & ANN: Let's get a plastic one!

ALL: *(They struggle to pick up large boxed Christmas trees,* **TAMMY** *and* **CHRIS** *complaining about the tackiness of plastic trees, their parents ignoring their complaints.)* By the window I think.

ALL: Decorations.

RAY & ANN: Lights, baubles…

TAMMY & CHRIS: … fairy.

RAY & ANN: It looks even better than the real ones.

TAMMY & CHRIS: Tacky, cheap and nasty muck.

RAY & ANN: If you don't stop being rude, Father Christmas won't come and see you!

TAMMY & CHRIS: *(Mock horror.)* Oh, no!

ALL: No more days till Christmas.

RAY & ANN: It's Christmas day.

TAMMY & CHRIS: *(To their own parents.)* Merry Christmas!

ANN: Merry Christmas, Chris.

RAY: Merry Christmas, Tammy.

ANN & RAY: *(Giving their child lots of presents)* Present. Present. Present.

TAMMY & CHRIS: Wow! Thanks!

ALL: Present. *(They exchange a present)* Thanks!

RAY & ANN: And that's not all. If you look over there you'll see …

TAMMY & CHRIS: *(Frantically unwrapping.)* Wow!!! A bike!!! Thanks Mum/ Dad.

RAY & ANN: And here's a little something extra!

TAMMY: A cool bicycle helmet. *(Immediately tries it on & does a catwalk turn.)* Does it suit me?

RAY: You look great, Tammy.

CHRIS: *(Disappointed.)* Mum. Do I have to wear it? It's gonna kill my hashtag swag!

ANN: Christopher!

CHRIS: Mum! Don't call me Christopher!

Section 2

CHRISTMAS OUTING

TAMMY: *(Wearing her helmet.)* Christmas afternoon, we both arrange to meet.

TAMMY & CHRIS: *(CHRIS enters, also his wearing helmet.)* "On yer bike at three o'clock at the bottom of the street."

CHRIS: "You'll miss the Queen do her speech!" me mum she says to me.
So, just to please her, I stay to watch it, then leave at ten past three.
"Now wrap up warm... don't want you to catch a chill...
And keep that cycle helmet on!"... "Yes Mum, course I will!"
But once her back is turned... I pull it off my head *(He does)* ...
It's alright... I won't fall off... I won't come back dead!!!

TAMMY: What kept you, Chris... no, don't tell me... your mum made you watch the Queen.

CHRIS: Don't be stupid... I was... er... giving my bike a clean.

TAMMY: *(Noticing the bike.)* New bike?

CHRIS: *(Noticing TAMMY's bike.)* New bike?

TAMMY: Blatantly!

CHRIS: Cool!

TAMMY: Sweet! So... why were you cleaning it?

CHRIS: Well, you know Aunt Ermintrude?

TAMMY: My favourite old Aunt...

TAMMY & CHRIS: ... with the knitting needles and the squeaky voice!

CHRIS: Yeah, well, I had to find some use for the home-made jumper she sent me.

TAMMY: Another one!

CHRIS: Yeah, this year it was yellow... with *(Inaudible.)* Winnie the Pooh sewn onto it.

TAMMY: With what?

CHRIS: Winnie the Pooh!

TAMMY: Nice! You'll never guess what she sent me.

CHRIS: I don't know… something cool.

TAMMY: Something super-cool.

CHRIS: I know you can't wait to tell me.

TAMMY: A new iPhone!

CHRIS: I don't believe it!

TAMMY: I can just imagine your mum… *(Mocking.)* "Ooh, isn't that smart. I know… you can wear that when you go to see Uncle Ray and Tammy on Boxing Day. Ooh! I will be proud!"

CHRIS: I've even got to write a thank-you letter… that's probably why she keeps sending them. She thinks I like them.

TAMMY: Tell her what a lovely colour it is… "Yellow… ooh! Lovely!" Vomit or what!

CHRIS: Hey, Tammy! Swap?

TAMMY: No way!

CHRIS: Worth a try!

TAMMY: Not really!

CHRIS: Come on… let's go to the park?

TAMMY: Whatever!

CHRIS: I'm not racing!

TAMMY: Didn't say you had to!

CHRIS: You were going to!

TAMMY: What **are** you on?

CHRIS: My new bike!

TAMMY: Ha ha! Funny!

TAMMY & CHRIS: *(Miming a bike ride.)* Riding to the park we see some mates from school

CHRIS: They can't believe the bikes we're on…

TAMMY: … then Chris shouts out …

CHRIS: Yo, dude!

TAMMY: Uncool!

CHRIS: Riding to the park, I think I'll do some tricks.
A wheelie, an endo and a double flick

TAMMY: Whack on the brakes and do a skid
"Chris has anybody told you you're a real sad kid!"

CHRIS: Yeah. *(Getting off imaginary bikes.)* But I'm changing! Today is not only Christmas Day… today is a turning point in my life. *(He starts to take on superhero persona.)*

TAMMY: A what?

CHRIS: The dawning of a new era.

TAMMY: What?

CHRIS: Hey you! I am a mean machine.

TAMMY: More like a micro machine!

CHRIS: Shut up!! I'm where it's at… I am where it's happening…
Christopher "super-hero" Simpson!

TAMMY: More like Christopher Robin with your friend Winnie the Pooh!
(Reminding him of jumper.)

CHRIS: And Gary "I think I'm a hero" Nelson had better watch out.

TAMMY: Why's that then, Chris?

CHRIS: He's always taking the mickey out of me and saying I'm rubbish at football.

TAMMY: Mate, I don't know how to tell you this, but you ARE a bit rubbish at football!

CHRIS: That's not the point! There's no need to keep on about it. He was having a right laugh about me with his girlfriend Linda Radcliffe.

TAMMY: Yeah, good one!

CHRIS: What do you mean?

TAMMY: Gary "I think I'm a hero" Nelson doesn't go out with Linda Radcliffe.

CHRIS: Yes he does!

TAMMY: No he doesn't, he dumped her last week.

CHRIS: How do you know?

TAMMY: I sort of made him do it! I said… "If you want to go out with me… you can't still be going out with her." – that's two-timing, isn't it.

CHRIS: You're going out with …

TAMMY & CHRIS: Gary "I think I'm a hero" Nelson!?

TAMMY: Yeah. It's Insta official!

CHRIS: *(Thinks about it.)* Urrrrrrrggggghhhhhh! That's disgusting. Why do you want to go out with him?

TAMMY: I like him. *(Seeing he is a bit upset.)* Don't worry Chris, you're still my cousin and best mate. *(Does something like tickling him to make him laugh.)* Mates?

CHRIS: *(He gives in and smiles.)* Come on let's go back to my place and…

TAMMY & CHRIS: *(Exaggerated mime to each other.)* … eat chocolate! *(They laugh)*

Section 3

A REPRIMAND FROM MUM

CHRIS's *house.* **CHRIS** *&* **TAMMY** *arrive home wearing helmets.*

ANN: *(In the Chirstmas spirit!)* Merry Christmas, Tammy!

TAMMY: Merry Christmas, Aunty Ann.

ANN: How were the bikes then?

TAMMY & CHRIS: Fine.

ANN: And the helmets?

TAMMY: Mine's cool.

ANN: What about yours, Chris?

CHRIS: Mine?

ANN: Yes. Yours.

CHRIS: You know what I think about mine.

ANN: I don't care what you think… as long as you wear it! *(Silence.)* You did wear it didn't you? Silence. Chris? *(Silence.)* Tammy… he did wear it, didn't he?

TAMMY: *(Quickly starting to exit.)* I'd better be going now, err, I've got to set up my new phone! It was my present from Aunt Ermintrude.

ANN: That was nice of her… she **made** Chris this lovely jumper, didn't she Chris?

CHRIS: Yeh, Mum. She did!

ANN: Anyway, Tammy, I asked you a question.

TAMMY: Didn't I give you an answer?

ANN: No you didn't!

TAMMY: Sorry… what was the question?

CHRIS: *(Suddenly shouts out.)* I didn't wear the stupid thing.

Silence. Everyone freezes.
(Quieter.) I look like a wally in it.

ANN: I will not tolerate being spoken to in that way in my house.

CHRIS: Shall we go to the garden then?

ANN: Christopher!

CHRIS: I'm not wearing it… not ever, no matter what you say!

ANN: Whatever has got into you?

CHRIS: You're always trying to make me look stupid. Kids at school still call me "Briefcase" because you made me go to school on my first day with some stupid leather briefcase…

ANN: It wasn't stupid, it belonged to your grandfather.

CHRIS: Exactly. You told me everyone at secondary school would have one!

TAMMY: Errrrm, is it alright if I go now, Auntie Ann?

ANN: Of course it is, Tammy. As soon as Christopher has apologised for being rude.

CHRIS: Oh, no, Mum please!

ANN: Christopher!

CHRIS: *(As insincerely as possible.)* Sorry, Tammy!

TAMMY: That's okay. See you tomorrow! "Christopher Robin!" *(She exits.)*

    CHRIS *is fuming and emits an involuntary noise to express that!*

ANN: Come here! *(He crosses to her apprehensively.)* What a fuss! What an embarrassment… and in front of Tammy too.

CHRIS: As if she cares!

ANN: I just want you to wear your cycle helmet. I don't understand why you have to be so awkward about it?

CHRIS: No one else wears them!

ANN: Tammy was wearing hers, wasn't she?

CHRIS: What difference does that make?

ANN: Your friend Gary Nelson wears one. I've seen him.

CHRIS: Number one… Gary Nelson is not my "friend".

ANN: He was!

CHRIS: Well he's not any more …

ANN: Oh I can't keep up with you and your friends …

CHRIS: *(Interrupting.)* And number two. Gary Nelson is sad!

ANN: He always looks happy enough to me!

CHRIS: *(Sarcastically.)* Ha ha ha! Mum, if you're cool… you don't wear them.

ANN: They all wear them in *Neighbours*.

CHRIS: *Neighbours* ain't cool… anyway they're in Australia…

ANN: What's that got to do with it?

CHRIS: They're all upside down over there!

ANN: *(Copying **CHRIS**.)* Ha ha ha! Your dad and I are agreed about this. If you want to use your bike, you've got to wear your helmet. And if you won't we'll just lock it in the garage until you change your mind.

CHRIS: Go on then!

ANN: Now you're being "sad"!

CHRIS: *(Creeping because he realises he is losing.)* Muuuuum. I'll do you a deal.

ANN: Try me.

CHRIS: I'll wear it… all the time… except for the journeys to and from school.

ANN: No! It's dangerous.

CHRIS: *(Imitating.)* "It's dangerous!" *(Normal voice.)* So is walking to school.

ANN: Not if you're sensible. You don't have to cross any main roads… not now they've built the subway. It's up to you. If you want to ride your bike anywhere you will have to wear your helmet. Your school should make it a rule. If everyone had to wear one, no one would take the mickey.

CHRIS: Well they won't. Our school only makes stupid rules.

ANN: So, you agree it is sensible. I know! I'll pop up to school at the beginning of term and have a word with your teacher about it. *(She exits triumphantly.)*

CHRIS: Mum! You're so embarrassing! Anyway you won't change my mind so you can lock it up where you like. It'll stay there and it'll never get used 'cos there's no way I'm going to wear the stupid thing. No way!

Section 4

VALENTINE'S DISCO

TAMMY: *(Both are wearing cycle helmets.)* Holidays fly by and soon we're back at school.

TAMMY & CHRIS: Riding our new bikes and feeling super-cool.

TAMMY: *(Taking off her helmet.)* Chris always wears his helmet now, I wonder what his mum said?

CHRIS: *(Taking off her helmet.)* It's got nothing to do with my mum…
I don't want a smashed up head!

TAMMY: When you wouldn't wear it, I thought you were really dumb…

CHRIS: Oh, stop going on, Tammy – you sound just like my mum!
(To audience) Tammy, she seems to have altered. She doesn't seem quite the same.
Mum says she's growing up too fast… and her boyfriend Gary's to blame!
Gary is a pain… he's going out with my best mate.
But I won't let him split us… Tam' and I shan't separate.

TAMMY: I get on well with Chris… he's my cousin and he's okay to me
But since I've been with Gary, it's him I want to see.
I see Chris every morning, but we don't talk much no more
I hate to dis him, but he is silly and immature.

TAMMY & CHRIS: February the fourteenth, our friendship seems to end.

TAMMY: Chris winds me up!

CHRIS: Tammy drives me round the bend!

TAMMY: It's over something so pathetic… a school Valentine's disco.
I mean, I promised Gary that I'd go with him, then Chris says to me
"You've got to make a choice! Him or me!"… like we were a couple or something!
He's trying to make me feel guilty, but I'll survive.
*(**RAY** enters silently behind **TAMMY** who remains unaware of his presence.)*

School discos are a laugh and I'm up for it. And I've only got half an hour to get ready! *(She mimes making up etc.)* Oh, I look awful!

RAY: You look great Tammy!

TAMMY: Hey, Dad! What's up?

RAY: Just wondering what time this disco finishes tonight?

TAMMY: Ten o'clock.

RAY: So you'll be home by ten thirty then?

TAMMY: No worries.

RAY: Is Gary picking you up?

TAMMY: No, we're meeting at the subway.

RAY: Hasn't there been some trouble there?

TAMMY: It's only Nut-Job.

RAY: Nut-Job?

TAMMY: Ian Sturrock… and his massive. They're just some Year 11's at school. They think they're hard, but they're not.

RAY: You be careful.

TAMMY: Course I will.

RAY: Is Chris going?

TAMMY: *(Laughing.)* He's not allowed.

RAY: Oh?

TAMMY: You know what Auntie Ann's like. *(Imitating.)* "I don't want my Christopher going to a disco. There'll be too many ruffians there and he'll end up in trouble! He's far too young for that kind of thing!"

RAY: Careful, that's my sister you're laughing at. Do you want a lift?

TAMMY: No, I don't want you embarrassing me.

RAY: As if I'd do that!

TAMMY: As if!

RAY: See you later. Don't forget. Ten thirty!

TAMMY: See ya! *(Exits in a hurry.)*

NUT-JOB: *(Entering loudly and announcing himself proudly.)* Nut-Job!

THE MASSIVE: Nut-Job's massive!

NUT-JOB: Where's the rest of the Massive?

THE MASSIVE: School disco.

NUT-JOB: Bah! Nut-Job…

THE MASSIVE: … and his massive

NUT-JOB: … don't do school discos. They like to watch people climb up the bank to cross the road to avoid Nut-Job…

THE MASSIVE: … and his massive!

NUT-JOB: Sometimes… some dudes tries to walk through Nut-Job's subway…

THE MASSIVE: … they don't try it twice…

NUT-JOB: … not if they value their life… not if they value eight pints of blood running through their veins…

THE MASSIVE: Nut-Job values his eight pints.

NUT-JOB: What's this?
Nut-Job spies some dude coming this way. Nut-Job strikes up a mean pose.

THE MASSIVE: … and so do his massive!

NUT-JOB: Nut-Job is a bit confused. This ain't no dude.

THE MASSIVE: This is a little Year 9 kid!

NUT-JOB: Nut-Job stands his ground and hollers:
Oi… You!

GARY: *(Innocently.)* Who me?

NUT-JOB: What's your name… little Year 9.

GARY: Gary Nelson.

NUT-JOB: Wrong!

THE MASSIVE: Wrong!

GARY: Eh?

NUT-JOB: Nut-Job's heard that your mates call you… Gary "I think I'm a hero" Nelson.

GARY: Wrong!

NUT-JOB: Wrong?

THE MASSIVE: Eh?

GARY: It's Gary "I am a hero" Nelson. *(He laughs nervously, which is not returned by* **NUT-JOB** *or* **THE MASSIVE**.*)*

NUT-JOB: Nut-Job thinks you're messing him around. Nut-Job wants to know who said you could pass through this subway… Nut-Job's subway?

GARY: I said I'd meet my girlfriend here.

NUT-JOB: *(Laughing.)* You've got a girlfriend?!

GARY: I'm afraid I have… sorry.

NUT-JOB: "Sorry"… is not good enough little Year 9. *(Picking* **GARY** *up by the scruff of his neck.)* Nut-Job wants you to beg for mercy and hand over all your money!

TAMMY: *(Entering. Sternly.)* No way, Gary!

NUT-JOB: Eh?

TAMMY: No way, Nut-Job. Put him down!

NUT-JOB: Tammy Eccles… the coolest girl on this manor. Nut-Job can't believe you're going out with him. *(He tries to make himself look attractive and saunters towards her.)* Hey babe – wanna go to the school disco with me?

TAMMY: *(Really assertively.)* No thanks – I'm going with my boyfriend. Come on, Gary! *(They walk through the subway to the amazement of* **NUT-JOB** *and* **THE MASSIVE**. *When they get to the other side they turn and face* **NUT-JOB** *again.)* Nut-Job, can't you find anything better to do than terrorise kids in Year 9…after all, it is… Valentine's night?

NUT-JOB: *(Suddenly low status and sad.)* Nut-Job hasn't got a date.

MASSIVE: No date – ha ha ha! *(Further reducing* **NUT-JOB***'s status.)*

TAMMY: Get a life, Nut-Job.

NUT-JOB: If you were a bloke, Nut-Job would sort you out proper!

TAMMY: Well, I'm not… so sling your hook, Nut-Job!

THE MASSIVE: Yeah, sling your hook!

NUT-JOB: Why don't you just get lost!

THE MASSIVE: No, you get lost!

NUT-JOB: No, you get lost!

THE MASSIVE: Do you know what? I'm off to the disco, where I've got FRIENDS! *(Exits maybe singing and dancing.)*

NUT-JOB: *(Beaten and alone.)* I didn't mean it! Come back! Please! *(Exits.)*

GARY: Well, now I've sorted him for you, I can give you this.

TAMMY: Gary! A red rose! How romantic. So… to the disco?

GARY: I can't wait!

TAMMY: You'll dance with me.

GARY: Course.

TAMMY: Even though your mates'll be there.

GARY: Tammy! I want them to see!

Sudden loud music and **TAMMY** *and* **GARY** *dance together. The audience can become involved in the dance routine too. After a while the music fades slightly for the following dialogue.*

GARY: Oh yeah, what did you say to Chris after school?

TAMMY: Why?

GARY: He was well upset.

TAMMY: I just got stressed with him… he can be such an idiot sometimes.

GARY: Maybe it'll do him some good… you know …

TAMMY: No, I was well over the top.

GARY: What did you say to him?

TAMMY: I was… I was a bit… well, really cruel. I'll phone him tomorrow… in the morning… We'll cycle to school together… get it sorted.

GARY: I'm sure he'll forgive you. I would.

They dance and laugh as the music fades, then suddenly **TAMMY** *spots the time.*

TAMMY: Gary… look at the time… eleven o'clock… my dad'll go mental!

GARY: He's sorted, your dad.

TAMMY: He is usually… but…

GARY & TAMMY: Come on… let's run!

TAMMY: I said goodnight to Gary at the corner of the street.
  The front room light's on… Dad's still up… so, I walk in… all discreet.
  (Enters.) What?! Dad's not in! What a relief… I thought I'd get loads of grief.
  At least he didn't have to wait… he'll have no idea that I was late.

RAY: I've been out looking for you!

TAMMY: What?

RAY: Looking at his watch. Ten past eleven… you said you'd be back by ten thirty.

TAMMY: It's only just after.

RAY: I rang your phone but you didn't answer.

TAMMY: It was on silent!

RAY: Anyway it doesn't take you an hour to get home from school.

TAMMY: *(With a wry grin.)* It did tonight!

RAY: I want to know where you've been, what you've been up to?

TAMMY: I haven't been "up to" anything!

RAY: I'm not stupid! You've must have been doing something.

TAMMY: Gary walked me home… I don't know… we were chatting.

RAY: Chatting! Tammy. For over an hour! I've been really worried.
  I've phoned the school and there was no one there.

TAMMY: Dad?

RAY: Don't you "Dad" me! Anything could have happened!

TAMMY: Whatever!

RAY: If you hadn't got back by midnight I was going to phone the police.

TAMMY: You often get home later than you say and I don't go phoning your office or telling the police.

RAY: That's different.

TAMMY: It's not!

RAY: If I stay on at work, it's to get enough money to make our lives more comfortable… and you know that!

TAMMY: But you're never here!

RAY: That's not the point… and it's not true! If you want to be treated like an adult you've…

RAY & TAMMY: *(Interrupting.)* … got to behave like one.

RAY: I wouldn't push it if I were you.

TAMMY: I'm off to bed.

RAY: Right! If that's all you've got to say, I'll ground you for the rest of the week …

TAMMY: No way!

RAY: And I'm not prepared to discuss it!

TAMMY: But Gary and me are going to the fair on Friday.

RAY: No, you were going to the fair.

TAMMY: Dad!

RAY: I can't imagine his parents'll be too happy about tonight either.

TAMMY: They won't mind… they probably won't even be in!

RAY: I'm not having this, Tammy.

TAMMY: You're just jealous! *(Immediately regrets saying this.)*

RAY: What do you mean?

TAMMY: Oh, it doesn't matter.

RAY: It does.

TAMMY: I'm off to bed.

RAY: Tammy! You said something. You can go to bed when you tell me what you mean.

TAMMY: *(Pause.)* You're just jealous 'cos you haven't got anybody. I'm sorry Dad, but it's true. *(Exits.)*

Section 5

THE ACCIDENT

CHRIS: Right since we were little kids, Tammy was my best mate
Did everything together… life was simple… we were great
Yesterday things changed… moved on… I don't really understand
So, today I'm off to school on my own… I don't need her to hold my hand.
I lift the garage door vowing "To Tammy I will not talk!"
(Sees his bike.)
Oh what! I've got a puncture… I'm gonna have to walk!
(Taking his mobile out of his pocket as he hears it ring, and not impressed to see **TAMMY**'s *name.)*

CHRIS: Tammy? What do you want?

TAMMY: Chris… I'm sorry about yesterday. Do you want to cycle to school with me?

CHRIS: I can't.

TAMMY: *(Resigned.)* Oh, alright. I just thought… you know …

CHRIS: I've got a puncture.

TAMMY: Shall we walk?

CHRIS: Seriously?

TAMMY: *(Sarcastically.)* I've never been so serious in all my life!

CHRIS: *(Looking at his watch.)* We'll have to run…

TAMMY: See you at the swings!

TAMMY & CHRIS: *(Suddenly together.)* Sorted!

Creating a different scene on the same stage.

LIZ: *(Calling out* **GARY**.*)* … Gary!

GARY: *(Off.)* What?

LIZ: It's half past eight.

GARY: *(Off.)* Where's Mum? Oh, Liz, why didn't you wake me up?

LIZ: What do you think I am doing?

GARY: *(Entering.)* I'll never get to school on time and we've got a test!

LIZ: A test, the day after a school disco? That's stupid!

GARY: Liz, can you give us a lift… please… you are the coolest sister anyone could ever have!

LIZ: *(Pretending to think about it.)* Ummmmmmm. *(Owning up.)* I was going to give you one anyway… Mum said you'd be tired so I should let you sleep in a bit. You want to get there in time for the test then?

GARY: Course I do! It'll be easy!

LIZ: Oh, will it now?!!

Back to the **CHRIS** *&* **TAMMY** *scene. She is carrying a balloon.*

CHRIS: *(Lively.)* Tammy, what are you doing with that balloon.

TAMMY: Gary gave it to me – it was from the disco.

CHRIS: *(Sarcastically.)* That's nice!

TAMMY: I think it's romantic.

CHRIS: Whatever!

TAMMY: Did you mind me phoning?

CHRIS: No… 's cool. How was it last night?

TAMMY: Awesome… you should have gone!

CHRIS: I would have done… if I was allowed.

TAMMY: My dad went mad with me after.

CHRIS: Why?

TAMMY: I got back late.

CHRIS: What time?

TAMMY: Quarter past eleven.

CHRIS: Tammy! What were you up to?

TAMMY: *(Conspiratorially.)* Do you really want to know?

CHRIS: Yeah.

TAMMY: Can you keep a secret?

CHRIS: Yeah!

TAMMY: Well after the disco, me and Gary were walking down the street, and he says, "Let's nick that car". So he breaks in, hot-wires it, and we're off down the road. Then he says "Let's ram raid the jewellers" so we crash into the front of it, Gary gets out, scoops up all the jewels and he gives me a hundred diamond rings!

CHRIS: *(Having been with the story all the way.)* Really?

TAMMY: No, silly! You'll believe anything! He just walked me home and we lost track of the time.

CHRIS: But the disco was good.

TAMMY: It was sorted!

CHRIS: Come on! We'd better get to school.

> *Cross to* **GARY** *&* **LIZ**… *now in a car…* **LIZ** *in the driving seat.* **GARY** *yawns.*

LIZ: Good night last night?

GARY: It was awesome!

LIZ: I bet it was, with Tammy! *(Laughing.)*

GARY: We've been going out for two months now! Do you think I look like a movie star?

LIZ: Why do you ask?

GARY: Just that Tammy thinks I do.

LIZ: Yeah, she probably meant Shrek!

GARY: I don't think so!

> *Back to the* **CHRIS** *&* **TAMMY** *scene.*

TAMMY: *(Pulling* **CHRIS**.*)* Come on, let's go and get some sweets.

CHRIS: Tammy!

TAMMY: Come on!

CHRIS: We're late as it is.

TAMMY: It's only registration. We can sign in late.

CHRIS: Alright. Tammy? Guess what? I'm making my debut for the school football team.

TAMMY: I know Gary said.

CHRIS: What did he say?

TAMMY: Just that… you were playing.

CHRIS: They won't have seen anything like it!

TAMMY: Yeah. *(Laughing to herself.)* Maybe he said that too!

CHRIS: What do you mean?

TAMMY: I thought you were in a hurry!

CHRIS: Eek! Yeah!

TAMMY & CHRIS: Ruuuuun… and into the shop… grab some sweets Pay at the checkout… and out onto the busy – *(They "mime" cars passing very fast.)* – very busy street.

Cross to **LIZ**'s *car.*

GARY: Come on, Liz… hurry up… they won't let me do the test today if I'm not there at the start.

LIZ: Course they will.

GARY: They won't. They've really tightened up since you went there.

LIZ: You're such a swot!

GARY: Just want to do well that's all.

LIZ: You mean you don't want to mess up like I did.

Back to the **CHRIS** *&* **TAMMY** *scene.*

CHRIS: It's raining! Let's run!

TAMMY: I'll race you.

CHRIS: No problem. *(They start running.)*

Cross to **LIZ**'s *car.*

GARY: If it keeps raining like this our football match'll be postponed.

LIZ: Who're you playing?

GARY: St Edmund's.

LIZ: You normally beat them.

GARY: We don't normally have "Briefcase" in goal for us.

LIZ: Why do you put a briefcase in the goal?

GARY: Not a real briefcase, it's this sad kid – actually he's Tammy's cousin! We could get hammered!

Back to the **CHRIS** *&* **TAMMY** *scene.*

CHRIS: Come on Tammy, cross here or we'll get drenched!

TAMMY: No…

CHRIS: Come on. Don't be such a chicken!

Cross to **LIZ***'s car.*

LIZ: Look at this rain!

GARY: Dad said I can have a fiver for every goal I score this season… he already owes me twenty quid.

LIZ: *(Holding out her hand.)* Petrol money.

GARY: No way! Dad always gets your petrol anyway!

LIZ: Only while I haven't got a job.

GARY: That's what I said… always!

LIZ: Cheeky!

Back to the **CHRIS** *&* **TAMMY** *scene.*

CHRIS: Time for Superhero Chris Simpson to strut out into the road, to dodge cars that dare to cross his path and slide past speeding motorcycles. He arrives at the other side of the road totally unscathed… adrenaline flowing… heart pounding… and ego… sky high! Yesss! Come on, Tammy. You try!

TAMMY: No. I'll use the subway.

CHRIS: "I'll use the subway"… don't be such a chicken.

TAMMY: It's not a matter of being a chicken…

CHRIS: What is it then?

Cross to **LIZ**'s *car.*

GARY: I'm getting a PS4 for my bedroom.

LIZ: How'll you afford that?

GARY: With the goal money from Dad.

LIZ: *(Laughing.)* You won't score that many goals!

Back to the **CHRIS** *&* **TAMMY** *scene.*

CHRIS: You're chicken. *(Taking out his mobile and starting to film* **TAMMY**.*)* It's official… Tammy is a chicken!

TAMMY: It won't come out… I'm too far away.

CHRIS: Wanna bet? I can show this to everyone.

TAMMY: No, Chris!

CHRIS: *(Meaning it.)* I dare you.

TAMMY: *(Thinks about it.)* Alright then.

CHRIS: Seriously?

TAMMY: Yeh. I'll make it worthwhile!

CHRIS: Come on then…

TAMMY: The cars were miles away when you crossed. See that red car…. I'll start when it reaches this lamppost.

VOICES: *A chant of "Chicken" is repeated rhythmically by the other actors to create an atmosphere of impending disaster/tragedy.*

CHRIS: Go on then… quick!

TAMMY: After the lamppost!

CHRIS: Do it!

TAMMY: No! *(***TAMMY** *hesitates, then finally steps in front of* **LIZ**'s *car.)* Now!

CHRIS: Tammy!

ALL: No!!!

TAMMY *is hit and falls. The balloon bursts.*

The staging of the accident should contain the main elements of this accident… i.e. impending danger, speed, screams/noise and impact.
Sudden silence.
Realisation sets in.

LIZ: Turn the music off, Gary.

CHRIS: I didn't think she'd do it.

LIZ: *(Disbelievingly approaching* **CHRIS**.*)* What was she playing at?

CHRIS: I don't know!

LIZ: *(In shock, hesitant but gaining in confidence.)* She just ran out in front of me… You must have seen something…

CHRIS: I didn't!

LIZ: Why would she do that?

CHRIS: I don't know! I don't know anything!

GARY: Liz! Liz! It's Tammy!

(Silence.)

CHRIS: While nobody was looking I slid my phone down a drain
I knew, if anybody found it I'd get the blame…
People'd say I'd encouraged her with a dare
They'd make judgements and think I didn't care
They'd say, I should've known better… should have been more mature
But, everyone knows… for one moment's stupidity, there is no known cure
Believe me… I'd do anything to change what happened that day.
When I saw Tammy's body on the dual carriageway…
Being totally covered by a blanket, then stretchered away…

*(***TAMMY*** and any other debris are cleared away. It is entirely acceptable for* ***TAMMY*** *to walk off stage with minimal fuss.)*

CHRIS: The funeral was awful, the church was packed. Everybody went.
I'll never forget her coffin, covered in the flowers that everyone'd sent.
Tammy's dad sat next to my mum… together in their grief.
She held his hand as the vicar talked of Tammy's life, saying it was "All too brief".
And then… then they played her favourite song and everyone cried.

Everyone apart from me… I felt numb. The truth in me had died.

GARY: *(Approaches* **CHRIS** *in silence.)* Chris… we should talk.

CHRIS: Should we?

GARY: I thought you might want to.

CHRIS: Well, you're wrong.

Silence.

GARY: Do you blame my sister, Chris? Is that why you won't talk to me?
Silence.
Liz wouldn't have been driving along that road if it wasn't for me…
so… so… was it my fault?

CHRIS: I'm not saying it was anyone's fault!

GARY: But others are… aren't they? That's the point. I didn't see
anything, nor did Liz and now people are starting to blame her. But
you were with Tammy, and you say you didn't see anything either but
surely… have you got any idea why she ran out like that?
Silence.
(Exasperated.) I'm just trying to… Oh, Chris, I'm sorry. *(Exits.)*

ANN: *(Entering.)* Chris, I've got you something. *(He looks up. She hands him a
carrier bag from a mobile phone shop.)* I know we said we wouldn't get you
another one but… well, it's been difficult for you… and well…aren't
you going to say anything?

CHRIS: *(Thrusting the phone back.)* Who do I phone now Tammy's gone…

ANN: Chris? How can you say such a thing?

CHRIS: Easily.

ANN: I thought you'd like it! I thought you'd be grateful. I should have
known better!
(He walks away.) Chris, I'm talking to you.
(Silence.)
You can't go on like this! It's been nearly a month since the accident
and you've hardly been out of the house. Your Head of Year called.
She wants you back in school on Monday.

CHRIS: I can't! Everybody'll… I can't face all the questions, Mum. I thought it'd end once the police had talked to me… but… there's kids at school and then there's the inquest… that won't be for ages either… and now you're starting… and there's something else. I can't cope with seeing Tammy's dad.

ANN: He's certainly not blaming you.

CHRIS: I know… he's been really kind… but… couldn't we move?

ANN: What?

CHRIS: Couldn't we move house… start again, away from everyone.

ANN: Then it really would look like you're running away from something.

CHRIS: But I'm not! I'm not! I just wish she hadn't done it.

ANN: I just wish someone had been there… you know… a witness… to see what happened… to see why she… I'm sorry, Chris. I don't really know what to do either… but you need to get back to some kind of normality…

CHRIS: Life will never be normal after this.

ANN: You know, Chris… sometimes I get the impression you are blaming yourself. It's not your fault. You were on the other side of the road. I mean… how could it be ever anything to do with you? *(Putting the package with the phone in front of him)* Chris… I'm not going to take this back. It will be useful. There will be people to talk to. There will be. I'm gonna leave it here *(She puts the unopened package down.)* You open it when you're ready. There's no rush. *(Makes a gentle physical contact with him. Exits.)*

CHRIS: *(Goes to exit, but then turns back to the audience.)* To this day I've not told anyone the words **you** know I said.

ALL: *(Offstage.)* Chicken!

CHRIS: Someone, somehow finding out is the one thing I most dread. I think about it every day, every night before I fall asleep.

It's a secret I must live with; a secret I must keep.

*The performer playing **CHRIS** should make a decision as to whether he opens the package containing the phone as music builds and the lights fade OR puts the package down unopened and exits. The performer is equally able to decide on a different option here that can be justified.*

Chicken! DVD/Download
StopWatch Theatre in Education Company
(Professional TIE Company)

This is the first of Mark's productions to be put onto DVD with professional performers. StopWatch Theatre Company has performed *Chicken!* nearly 6,000 times since 1992 from Cornwall to the Shetland Islands. Their outstanding production is filmed in front of two Year 6 audiences (edited into one performance), to give an unprecedented opportunity to study a high quality professional TiE production in action.

The DVD includes:

Chicken! by Mark Wheeller, performance of the play
by 2M/2F professional cast

Follow-up Workshop, the acclaimed StopWatch Theatre Company workshop which examines decision making and assertiveness
for KS2 audiences

Interview with Mark Wheeller (writer) and Adrian New (director),
the story of the development of *Chicken!*

Interview with the Cast, an insight into the life of actors in a TiE company.

In light of this recent announcement from BTEC this DVD/download will provide opportunities to study Wheellerplays:

*'You'll be pleased to hear that we will allow Mark Wheeller's plays
to be used in Component 1 of the Tech Award. If it has recordings of
a professional, student or youth theatre production that you can access,
you are free to select it for use in Component 1.'* Paul Webster

Bonus Features:

One of Mark's most recent plays, *Chequered Flags to Chequered Futures.*
Presented by Victoria Shanghai Academy in Hong Kong who commissioned it.

Mark describes *Chequered Flags* as his most mature verbatim RTA play with a fascinating structure and some amazingly powerful monologues for a female performer. Also, a Q & A with playwright Mark Wheeller, the director, Joanna Crimmins and the Gilfoy family (central characters in the play). Chris Gilfoy developed the role of Chris in the original production of *Chicken.*
Available from Salamander Street.

Teachers – if you are interested in buying a set of texts
for your class please email info@salamanderstreet.com
– we would be happy to discuss discounts and keep you up
to date with our latest publications and study guides.

Missing Dan Nolan
Paperback 9781913630287
eBook 9781913630294

Chequered Flags to Chequered Futures
Paperback 9781913630355
eBook 9781913630348

Game Over
Paperback 9781913630263
eBook 9781913630270

Hard to Swallow
Paperback 9781913630249
eBook 9781913630256

Too Much Punch For Judy
Paperback 9781913630300
eBook 9781913630317

Hard to Swallow, Easy to Digest
(with Karen Latto)
Paperback 9781913630409
eBook 9781913630393

Hard to Swallow, Easy to Digest: Student Workbook
Paperback 9781913630416
eBook 9781913630423

The Story Behind … Too Much Punch for Judy
Paperback 9781913630379
eBook 9781913630386

Salamander Street will be publishing new editions of Mark's plays
in 2020 – follow us on Twitter or Facebook or visit our website
for the latest news.

www.salamanderstreet.com

9 781913 630331